# Quiz Night

Written by
**Rob Waring** and **Maurice Jamall**

# Before You Read

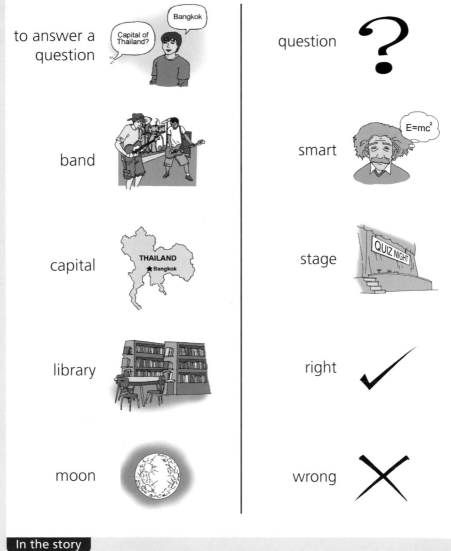

to answer a question — Capital of Thailand? Bangkok

question — ?

band

smart — E=mc²

capital — THAILAND ★ Bangkok

stage — QUIZ NIGHT

library

right — ✓

moon

wrong — ✗

## In the story

Gemma    Ji-Sung    John    Mr. Becker    Daniela

"There's a Quiz Night, next Saturday," says Daniela.
Ji-Sung, John, and Daniela are looking at a poster.
"Ji-Sung, are you going to be in the Quiz Night? You're
very smart," says John.
Daniela says, "Yes, you can win some pizza tickets, too."
"Yes, I think I'll go," says Ji-Sung. "I can win. And then
I'll give you some pizza."
"Wow, thanks," says John. "I *love* pizza!"

Daniela asks, "John, are you in the Quiz Night?"
"No, I'm helping with the questions," he says. "Mr. Becker and I are making the questions for the Quiz Night. We're going to the library tomorrow afternoon," he says.
"Wow, that's great, John," says Daniela. "Don't make the questions too difficult!"
A girl is watching them. Her name is Gemma.

The next day, Mr. Becker and John are in the library. They are making questions for the Quiz Night. Gemma comes to them. She knows they are making the questions.

"What are you doing?" she asks.

Gemma tries to look at the questions. But Mr. Becker puts his paper under a book.

"We are making questions for the Quiz Night. Please don't look," says Mr. Becker.

"Oh, sorry," she says.

Later Gemma sees John. She asks, "John, do you want some money?"

"No. Why?" asks John.

"Give me the questions and answers for the quiz," says Gemma.

John is very surprised. "No, I will *not* give you the answers. Go away!" says John.

"Come on, John. It's okay, nobody will know," says Gemma.

"No! No! And no again!" says John. He's angry with Gemma. He doesn't like her.

It is Saturday, and it is Quiz Night. There are six people. They all want to win.

Mr. Becker says, "Let's start. All the players will answer some questions. One wrong answer and you are out. Do you understand?" he says. Everybody understands.

John gets the first ball.

"The first question is for Yoon-Hee," says Mr. Becker. A tall girl answers the first question. Yoon-Hee is Ji-Sung's sister.

"Yoon-Hee, what's the name of the first man on the moon?" Mr. Becker asks.

Yoon-Hee answers, "Yuri Gagarin."

"No, I'm sorry, Yoon-Hee, that's the wrong answer," says Mr. Becker. "It's Neil Armstrong. You are out."

"Sarah, what's the name of the writer of the *Harry Potter* books?" he asks.

She answers, "I don't know. Is it Anita Rodling?"

"No, I'm sorry, it's not. It's J.K. Rowling. Sorry, you're out, too," says Mr. Becker.

Mr. Becker asks Gemma the next question.
"Gemma, what's the name of the tall tower in Paris?"
"It's the Eiffel Tower," she says.
Mr. Becker says, "That's right!"
"The next question is for Ji-Sung. Ji-Sung, where are the Petronas Towers?" he asks.
Ji-Sung answers, "They're in Kuala Lumpur, in Malaysia."
"That's right!" says Mr. Becker.

Mr. Becker asks Ji-Sung the next question.
"Which British rock band sings the song *Yesterday*, Ji-Sung?
"Is it The Beatles?" answers Ji-Sung.
Mr. Becker says, "That's right. Okay. Now, the next question."
"Mark, the White House is in the United States. Where's the
Blue House?" asks Mr. Becker.
"Is it in India?" asks Mark.
"No, I'm sorry it's not. It's in South Korea. I'm sorry, you're out,"
says Mr. Becker.

Gemma and Ji-Sung are very good. They get all their questions right.

"Gemma, what's the capital of Vietnam?" asks Mr. Becker.

"It's Hanoi," says Gemma.

Mr. Becker says, "That's right!"

"Ji-Sung, which two languages do people speak in Canada?" he asks.

"English and French," Ji-Sung says.

"Very good!" says Mr. Becker.

John talks to everybody. He says, "Well, there are only two people, Gemma and Ji-Sung. Who will win?" he asks.
He says, "We'll now listen to some music. We'll start the questions again in ten minutes."
Ji-Sung and Gemma go to their friends. John does not want Gemma to win. He wants to help Ji-Sung. John comes to talk to Ji-Sung.

JUNIOR QUIZ NIGHT

John says, "Ji-Sung, what's the capital of Thailand?"
"It's Bangkok," Ji-Sung answers. "Why do you ask?" he asks.
"Oh, you know that!" says John. "It's okay."
Ji-Sung asks, "John, why are you asking?"
"It's the next question," John replies.
"What? It's the next question? Oh no!" he says. "I can't win now!"
"But, you know the answer . . . ," says John.
"Yes, but I know the question!" Ji-Sung says. He is very angry with John.

Ji-Sung goes back to the stage. He is looking at John. He is very angry with him. He is waiting for his question.

Mr. Becker asks, "Ji-Sung, what's the capital of Thailand?"

Ji-Sung looks at John and says, "I don't know!"

John is very surprised. "What's Ji-Sung doing?" he thinks. "He knows the answer! I don't understand."

Mr. Becker asks, "Gemma, what's the capital of Thailand?"

"Bangkok!" she says.

"Gemma's the winner!" says Mr. Becker. "Congratulations!"

Ji-Sung goes back to his friends. He is very angry with John.
"It's okay," says Mark.
"Bad luck," says Daniela.
"That's okay," says Ji-Sung. "I can't win everything! What do *you* think, John?" he asks.
"Yes, you're right," John says. John puts his head down and everyone looks at him. His face is very red.

"Let's all go and get some pizza," says Daniela.

Yoon-Hee says, "Okay, good idea! Let's go everybody."

"Umm. . . , I'm not coming," says John. Everybody looks at John. They are surprised.

"But you love pizza, John!" says Daniela.

John looks at Ji-Sung. "I'm not hungry now," he says.